The Happy Clown

Warren Padla

Print information available on the last page

Rev. date: 06/14/2017

To order additional copies of this book, contact:
Xlibris
1-888-795-4274
www.Xlibris.com
Orders@Xlibris.com

The Happy Clown

Warren Padla

This book is dedicated to my lifelong companion Charles Talluto

Contents

The Bee

One summers day in mid-July, I sauntered down a rocky path, secluded and forbidding;
the trees and vines were on all sides, entangled, strong, and hidden;
I trudged along the darkened path with fear for one full hour,
with help, of course, from filtered light shone down into the bower;
not knowing where the path would lead my thoughts all turned to leaving,
when all at once the darkness left and sunlight came down streaming;
the trees were gone and in their place were flowers everywhere;
at left, at right, way down the road, a paradise with flair;
and then I heard a buzzing sound and turned around to see,
a gorgeous sight of color rich, a flower and a bee;
his wings were moving at great speed in sunshine bright and blazing,
with yellow colors mixed with white, it really was amazing
I stood transfixed and mystified, and moved a little closer;
it didn't phase him in the least to have an interloper;
when all the garden work that he had done was finally finished,
he took to flight and flew towards me with buzzing undiminished;
he circled round my head three times and never did I cower,
then off he flew into the breeze, to find another flower.
Entranced and dazed and mystified, with tears upon my face,
I headed back to home, renewed, refreshed, and in a state of grace.

The Old Vine

The red brick wall was old and cracked,
but still was strong and active;
all covered by a tough old Vine
that made the wall its captive.
Each year in Spring,
the vine grew leaves of green and tiny flowers,
a beauty even more when hit with April showers.
Blue birds would join the Vine each year
to do their season's nesting,
and live there till their newborn babes
had finished all their testing;
then off they'd fly into the sky in search of lofty places,
with fondest memories of the Vine and all its many graces.

The Storm

The Storm was fierce with deadly winds that pointed to a farmland,
that once was filled with life, and love, a farmer's precious homeland;
but droughts had hit and done their deeds, and things began to die,
and all the prayers to no avail brought water from the sky.
The farmer's plight was very sad, and caused a flood of grieving,
and many poor almost broke, had frequent thoughts of leaving;
but then the winds dug up a path that headed north and went upon its way,
and formed what looked to some, quite clear, a perfect water way.
With winds all passed, silence returned except for one soft calming sound;
a strange and gushing noise it was, like music all around.
The sad old farmers all came out to see the Storm's real damage,
but all they saw was one long trench, and things that they could manage.
And then the gushing sound grew loud, and eyes all turned,
to view the northern mountain, and down it came, all
fresh and clean, like water from a fountain.
The farmers shocked and filled with joy in this their golden hour,
gave thanks and praise unto the Storm and to the Higher Power.

Scarola

This precious leafy lettuce green is much less known than others,
but beats them all by very far, for all the field it covers;
Its greatest use turns out to be, a must for one good salad,
and praises for its taste are surely very valid;
but then it makes a lovely soup that simply is delicious,
and more impressive is the fact, that it is so nutritious;
but last of all, sautéed with oil and garlic lightly toasted,
it hits the charts and gets high marks, and freedom to be boasted.

The Indian Sign

The town is known as Williamsville; It's just a tiny hamlet,
with one small green, on one small street with only seven houses;
but long ago was home to Indians, their children, and their spouses.
In honor of this peaceful tribe, a sign of them was painted;
it showed a Chief with bow in hand, like ones that we're acquainted.
The sign stood firm for many years, and was the town's proud treasure;
its value as a prized antique was one that had no measure.
One late dark night in early spring, the sign was quickly taken,
and when the folks all learned the truth, they were so badly shaken.
The folk grew sad as time went by, and some lost all their hope,
until a plan was made one day, of quite a different scope.
The plan was such that all the folk would meet upon the green,
and offer prayers to ONE above, kneeled down, and quite unseen.
Their prayers were said for hours long, with just a single thought,
that he who took the sign from them, would feel the hurt he wrought.
Some days went by, and jokes were made, and many thought it foolish,
and even more than that mean act, some even felt it ghoulish.
Until one foggy early morn when sun returned good light,
there lay the sign upon the posts, dropped off within the night.
The folk all gathered once again, relieved from sadness and their cares,
and offered thanks to ONE above, who answered all their prayers.

The Breeze

Across a sleepy low lit stream,
a quiet breeze swept by;
It made its way across the land,
determined and unshy;
It covered flowers, rocks, and sand,
and all within its path,
with tiny droplets wet and cool,
a shower, soft and daft;
Worn out at last from miles of flight,
it fell to earth and out of sight;
But left behind were gifts of life,
like grass, like trees, like flowers;
A mighty tribute to the Breeze,
for all its final hours.

The Red Carnation

She tiptoed lightly down the stairs, so quietly and some pause
At only eight, it was quite clear, her sight was on a cause
Her mother's drawing pad, her brushes, and her paints;
her goal to leave behind a painting, large, simple, and quite quaint
She sat right down upon the chair and readied several brushes,
and then began her first art try, with red and white paint touches
The piece became a flower, large, like one giant red carnation,
and in all truth, the finished piece, was really a sensation
She tiptoed lightly up the stairs and went back to her room,
and wished the day would start again, and very very soon
The time went slow and seemed like years but finally it arrived;
her mother planned to paint that morn, the artist had survived
Her mother walked in nonchalant and headed for her chair,
but noticed something on her board, bright colors and real flair
She knew at once who did the piece and called her loud and clear,
to come right down without delay to praise her with good cheer
The rest is history in the Arts, a story of belief,
the lass who did the fl ower then, became the great O' Keefe.

A Sailor's Story

A sailor's story lingers long while others disappear; its locale point is Cuban soil when freedom was still here. My tall young frame was all decked out with new tight tailored whites, with thirteen shiny buttons new, that much improved the sight. With nineteen years, a handsome face, and soft gold flaxen hair, this sailor boy was sure this day that he could spin a lair. With shipmates at my side as well, we headed for a bar, an outside Tiki bar we found, that was not very far. We took a table near a band then playing Cuban songs, and ordered lots of beer and food, that quickly came along. Some senoritas sitting close to us sent smiles that lit the sky; it didn't take us long to know, they were not very shy. My dancing skills kicked in real soon with one who sat nearby, and soon we ruled the whole dance floor, like angels from the sky. We danced and danced, and never stopped, it was a sight to see; a lovely senorita doll and sailor all aglee. The hours passed and music ceased, but love had hit my heart; so soon the scene became a room, two cocktails for a start. There was a kiss, but after that, all life in me went blank, and on the wooden floor within that room, my body slowly sank. When life came back and I awoke, my valuables were missing, and so the same was true, the girl that I was kissing. I ran with fear through dark lit streets and made it to the dock, in time to board my ship alive, but in a state of shock. As years rolled on the story stayed as clear as yesterday, and now it's down on paper stock and long will be its stay.

The Visit

A sound sleep ends with sounds of wings and tiny crashes of small things; my eyes roam round the room to search the scene, and soon I know it's not a dream. And then the wings take flight again from bedroom out the door; I get right up and follow it, still nervous to the core. The next door room is my small den that's always warm and bright, so easy is it now to see the stranger that took flight. Upon a tiny lamp, dim lighted is a shade, and thereupon my eyes could see a tiny bird, afraid. I slowly moved towards him, while keeping down my pace, and he seemed calm as one could be, in such a foreign place. With index finger as a post, I raised it to his feet; his eyes looked on at every move and never missed a beat. And then he calmly hopped upon the post, gave out a quiet beep, and seemed to trust his host he wakened from a sleep. I then walked towards my terrace door with birdie hanging on, and stepped outside real slow, not causing an alarm. Outside, he gave out with a few more chirps and I expected flight, but my new friend seemed quite at ease, and reluctant to take flight. I had the nerve to move my lips close up to his small beak, and he stayed put, and gave a gentle peck to me upon my cheek. And then with that he took to flight and headed on his way, and so enchanted was I then, I kneeled right down to pray. I thanked the Higher Power up above for all the birds that fly, and ended prayer that mystic day still focused on the sky.

The Mighty Maple

Tiny droplets from the tap;
perfect timing of the sap.
Trees' free gifts of God's great bounty;
wooden buckets in every county.
Then to kitchen and to table,
a syrup known for years, since cradle.
And golden color everywhere,
lights up the trees with firing flair.
Next, leaves depart and feed the earth
and maple seeds insure rebirth.
Tiny droplets from the tap;
perfect timing of the sap.

True Friendship

Like the moon can cause the waves to move,
and Sun can grow the flowers,
So too, a friend can fill another's life with many golden hours.
So strive your best to sow True Friends through love,
through trust, through duty, so in the later years of Life,
each day is filled with beauty.
True friendship, immortal as the Soul,
lives on and on forever,
and neither man nor death from you,
this gift, can either ever sever.

The Happy Clown

When lights go out within your life,
and all your world grows dark;
strike out with steel on solid rock
until you see the sparks.
Then burn the candles in your mind,
and bring in fresh new light,
while wiping sadness in your eyes,
forever from your sight.
Then open all the windows wide
and sing a happy song,
and treat yourself, and friends as well,
to gifts for which you long.
Then paste a joyful smile upon your face,
and never wear a frown;
make Life a Circus every day,
and You, the Happy Clown.

Grey To Blue

Blue skies in one's life can often turn grey,
and cloud up one's vision for quite a long stay.
You falter and stumble in things that you do,
and why it is happening, you haven't a clue.
Your life seems to wallow in sadness and gloom,
and thoughts of the future all focus on doom;
but when least expected, soft lighting comes in,
and causes the grey in your life to grow dim;
all color turns quickly to quite a bright blue,
and dreams that you had of good life, all come true.
You think of the trials in your life that seemed long,
and know now that all of the trials made you quite strong;
you make it your duty to spread the good news.
how life once all greys, is now all bright blues.

The Olde Wooden Rocker

The olde wooden rocker was rustic and worn; no one could remember the year it was born. It rocked with one partner for decades of years but now it was silenced and all were in tears. The faithful old rider had ended her ride and all who stood nearby were silent or cried. The rocker stood empty for one or two years, when something strange happened and filled all with fear. A storm had arisen and hit the old house, and doors were all opened by wind from the South. The wind hit the rocker and it started to move, a back and forth motion, not fast, just real smooth. The storm kept its force for about one full hour, and then left, worn out with almost no power. The house in a short time was brought back to order but one thing remained that is hereby recorded. The rocker kept rocking, and rocking away, and nothing could stop it or stand in its way. Some folks say its rocking right up to this day, but most feel this gossip is merely heresay. But miracles happen and old legends live on, and so will the old rocker long after we're gone.

CPSIA information can be obtained
at www.ICGtesting.com
Printed in the USA
BVHW021150280219
541438BV00009B/87/P

* 9 7 8 1 5 4 3 4 2 8 1 0 0 *